Livin' La Vida Lockdown

Introduction

Okay...so, I was thinking, a while back, in the wake of recent events, that this was something that *had* to be written. I haven't *quite* figured out *why* as yet, but, well, inspiration strikes at strange moments, and I got the title for the work after seeing Ricky Martin's music video of *Livin' La Vida Loca* once too often on the *That's T.V* music channel! (Got me thinking about parodies, you see!) And I guess I needed an escape from this perpetual hell that we shall call a *pandemic*, for now!

At the time of kicking this off, I'm not entirely confident that we are out of the woods as yet, as I am of the opinion that mad exiguous viruses are a lot like bills...you're never free of them! Just when you think you have everything sussed, or whatever term you're at home with, something else comes along to knock you for six!

Right, so, *this* little number is all about chronicling the pandemic, in layman's terms, from where it all began, to where we are *now*. It's said that history is written by the victors, but, I have no personal issues as there are no winners or losers here. However, I have to warn you that personal bias may creep in from time to time, as this is unavoidable, given that it's *me* relating everything, to the best of my knowledge, to *you*. Be prepared for us to lock horns on *some* things, and link arms on *others*! Glad to have you aboard!

L Tait.

February 2021

<u>*Genesis*</u>
<u>*(Not The Band!)*</u>

So...one of the many unanswered questions...how did it all begin?
Accounts vary, from bats, to pangolins, animal to human transmission in *true* avian flu stylee, but, one solid fact is that it all happened in China, more specifically, Wuhan province. When it was first reported by concerned scientists and medical experts in the area, the government was super, *Hush, Hush, Sweet Charlotte* about it...not the reaction you'd expect upon the discovery of something that was set to take the world by storm. and, *not* in a *good* way, unlike *The Masked Singer*! You get my meaning! To the point of making claims that there was limited human to human

transmission too. But, once admissions were reluctantly made that it was highly likely that human transmission was imminent...it was too late, and far too evident to suppress! The pandemic was on its way round the world! The first recorded cases of what was later named, COVID-19, in the U.K were in March 2020, although I am very much of the opinion it was on Blighty round about November or December 2019. The reason for this, is down to my profession. We had started stocking face masks around that time, as we had seen an unexpectedly huge demand for them, among members of that particular community, so something was up, back then. Even *more* surprising, on the reactionary front, was that, despite the growing prevalence of this mystery disease, China still held its new year celebrations! As one government minister later said, 'Covid loves a crowd.' Well, I just bet it was partying hard among the revellers! That quote should have gone on a t-shirt! Having watched a Channel 4 documentary not long ago about all this, my synapses started firing off when I saw that, right on the doorstep of the wet market in Wuhan province, where this virus had allegedly originated, there was a laboratory! As the song goes, it's one of those, *Things That Make You Go Hmmm*! Visions of an experiment that went wrong, and the incriminating evidence being destroyed amid that wet market, where it couldn't be traced back to a scientific facility, suddenly didn't seem all that implausible to me! All of those animals to choose from! Which one to pick? It didn't bear the hall marks of a noble attempt at a catchall for a cure all ills, with a Nobel prize in the offing! No way dot com! When it comes to claiming *credit* for anything, humans will behave like crabs in a bucket! Even to get just a smidgeon of praise, they will trample all over each other in a mad stampede to get the reward! But...whenever a *disaster* occurs, like, I don't know, say, a *pandemic,*resulting in the deaths of *millions* of people, not to mention those who have ended up with 'long covid', and permanent damage to their organs, the human misery of social restrictions (more on *that* later!), economic fallout, among other things, *nobody*, I repeat, *nobody* will *ever* admit to having a hand in *that*! It shows great courage to own up to making a mistake at your work, but it's a whole other act when your actions have caused *that* much damage! For what it's worth, my guess is the person responsible has disappeared, or is dead, possibly hoisted by their own petard, or, blown up by their own covid bomb! And...so it began!

Arrival
(Not The ABBA Song!)

When COVID-19 hit the U.K, the respective governments were all so very...*British* about it! Maybe, just maybe, if they ignored it for long enough, it would go away! No cause for alarm folks! Everyone go back to your homes, nothing to see here! However, *that* approach could only last for so long, before the disease decided it *wouldn't* be ignored, via the case numbers! And, as the numbers ascended, and resources grew more and more scarce, the powers that be decided to control the population! Enter, drumroll please, *Lockdown* 2020! Now, this was not entirely a new concept! We'd seen it on shows like *Pointless*, and *The X Factor*, so...*where,* exactly, did the GBP (the Great British Public) feature in this scenario? We were as much in the dark about it as the governments were, and, come to think of it, still are! It's not like they weren't prepared for it, or didn't see it coming! Bearing in mind that the batting average for a pandemic is every hundred years, give or take, and the *last* one occurred in 1920, we were due another one, weren't we? It's the historical imperative! There was no getting out of *this* one unscathed! Maybe the pandemic was karmic payback for all the money that *should* have been used to fund the National Health Service, that mysteriously went elsewhere. I read somewhere that, in total, the NHS had been screwed over by administrations, past and present, for *nine years*, under what they called

'austerity measures.' Now, I'm all for saving money as much as the next person, but I am of the opinion that, sometimes, you really *can't* save money, under certain circumstances. Money has to be spent where it's truly needed, to offset a greater expenditure later on. Why not pay to get a few roof tiles replaced, if it's going to save you the price of an entire *roof*? So...was it *really* in the best interests of the government to skip out on nine years worth of funding, when you count the cost of the pandemic to date? What makes it even worse, is that we'll be continuing to pay for the pandemic for a long time to come! We might still be paying for it when the *next* pandemic comes!
In *fact*, I'd put money on it! But, I'm not planning on living that long!
And so, Bojo the clown (my favourite soubriquet for the current Prime Minister of this many sceptered isle!), on the 23rd of March 2020, sat down at No10, and addressed the nation! We were officially going into Lockdown! What did that even *mean*? Read on!

Lockdown...2020

So, it came to pass that life, as *we* knew it, would be radically changed, albeit temporarily. And, how we received this news was very telling! Glued to our television screens, this latest turn of events, for most, prompted the general reaction of, 'This is *history*! We'll be a part of a major historical event! Wait till we tell the grandchildren about *this*!'The new and the unfamiliar always has a certain cache...until the novelty wears off, and, closing in on almost a *year* since the announcement of the *first* lockdown, I'd say we were all getting more than a *little* weary of the whole thing!

Using an olde worlde model of how Britain approached the 1920 Spanish Flu pandemic, it was officially announced that all 'essential', (in the eyes of the government anyway) businesses were to close, and so the 'furlough'scheme was born! This was designed to offset job losses, where the government paid a whopping eighty percent of the wages of staff that had to stay home, with the employer footing the bill for the remaining twenty percent. Nice work if you can get it! It didn't exactly help out the employees who were automatically made redundant when the lockdown went on for far longer than first thought, and, as far as the government picking up the tab was concerned, they were using taxpayers'money to do it! The same taxpayers'who would be repaying the loan as it were, for years to come! Meanwhile, schools were also to close, so that meant a lot of bored children and teenagers were destined to be stuck at home, because all the fun places had been shut down too! The government very generously allocated a whole hour a day devoted to exercise, but, as the parks were closed, this meant the streets became very cluttered up with aimless souls, not used to having so much free time, and having nowhere to spend it. Public transport services were completely pared back, a nightmare if you had mobility issues or were a 'key' worker solely reliant on it to get you where you needed to be. Benches at train stations were all covered in tape like something out of a crime scene, just to prevent people sitting on them, such was the fear that COVID survived on hard surfaces! Flour became hard to get, as there was an uptick in parents trying to amuse the children at home by teaching them to bake. As the gyms were closed, there was also a huge number of joggers out and about. Like tripping over everyone else who had nowhere else to go wasn't bad enough! As the situation was all so very new, we didn't know what to expect from it, so we rolled with it.

However, just as there were people on furlough, getting paid to stay at home and be bored senseless, safe in the knowledge that their job would be waiting for them, there were also people who *had* to go out and work, to keep the country going during this difficult time! Let's give a round of applause for the *key* worker, later dubbed, *critical* worker! Mostly minimum wage shills in the service industries and health sectors, who *couldn't,* 'Stay home, stay safe, protect the NHS'Nope, their lot in life was to either, go out and work, with the additional risk of COVID thrown into the mix, or, ' stay home and starve.'The agony of *choice*! Suddenly, these previously unsung heroes who'd been classed as posessing little to no skills, hence the minimum wage, had been elevated to superhero status!Who would have thought the humble supermarket cashier or pharmacy dispenser (me!) would be so fundamentally important to the country during a pandemic? We *really* didn't see *that* coming, did we? We should be receiving our knighthoods any day now!

The Early Days

I felt that we needed a little bit of context, so, I'm going to take you back in time to the days leading up to the lockdown. Now, some people out there, before the announcement, were, how shall I put it, getting their ducks in a row! Let's call it what it is! Panic buying! From my own side, my workplace had never seen so many people pass through its doors in such a short space of time! The products most in demand were, sanitiser, face masks and gloves. People were actually queuing up to get in! This wasn't the only place where I'd seen so much panic! I was also in Farmfoods, behind a massive queue of people, and everyone in the queue had a big multipack of toilet roll! I kid you not, people! People just went absolutely crazy! Even the store where I can usually get an online shopping slot with just a couple of days notice, were booked solid! So, I found myself doing my shopping old school, carrying it in bags to the bus stop (as there were next to no trains running)and carrying it home! It's not an experience I'd like to repeat. Besides, you probably guessed that I don't drive! But, I would *love* to! Online reports showed empty shelves, and some supermarkets were limiting products too! With such pandemonium at large, it was only a matter of time before the government got involved, and, get involved they did. Things could have got pretty scary if they hadn't introduced some sort of system. And so, the Soviet Russia system was brought into existence! I totally get that, in *some* situations, you need to stand in a queue! Cinema, club, sweet counter at the cinema, checkout at the supermarket, and so on. But, I'll bet you *anything* you never expected to have to queue up to get *into* a shop! Am I *right*? I'm not *wrong*! And...off the back of this all new queuing concept, came the bizarre phenomenon we have all come to know, and consequently, *loathe*, as, wait for it...*Social Distancing*!(pause for applause!). I have *never*, in the whole history of my immediate universe, understood the concept as, when one thinks of all things *social*, one thinks about get togethers, parties, human warmth, compassion, interaction, closeness, intimacy, the whole box and dice. And yet...when you *really* get on down to the nuts and bolts of it all, like the term, 'Company loyalty', it's a complete contradiction of terms! We really should start brainstorming about finding some sort of umbrella term that could cover such banal, inane, and zany ideas! I'll get the ball rolling here! 'Contradictions!'So, what have *you* got? Probably something better! It's a work in progress! Anyway, to the uninitiated, (and I very much doubt there are any out there, unless you've been living under a rock for near enough the past year!), there is nothing *remotely* (see what I did there?) 'social'about it! Aside from it relating to 'society'in the thematic sense, it ticks no other boxes for me! I have a *much* more fitting soubriquet for you all! Hang on to your hats, people! My own personal favourite...*Antisocial Distancing*! You can dress it up in any other language you *like*, but, that's what it *is*! When you *really* think about it, this is *exactly* what it promotes! How *else* could you describe maintaining a two metre distance between yourself and others around you, wherever you *go*, whatever you *do*, no hugging, touching, hand shaking, even with the people you know and *love*? Acting like someone you pass in the street might have this perpetual, proverbial plague, so you give them a massive body swerve, instantly making them feel as distrustful of *you* as you *appear* to be of *them*? Doesn't sound very 'social' to *me*! That has been something of a bugbear in my world of late, having to unpick socially accepted norms that have been a part of the fabric of our existence for *centuries*, in a mere matter of *weeks*! What is *wrong* with the universe? Seems like everything is down to *money*! Yes, because the money didn't go where it was *supposed* to go, the government, in its infinite wisdom, decided that, instead of shoring up the NHS funding, they'd have *much* more fun controlling society, and putting the blame on *us,* making us, the taxpayers, essentially, *pay* for *their* mistakes! There's gratitude for you! ' So long, and thanks for all the fish!' to quote the dolphins from *The Hitchhiker's Guide To The Galaxy*. (Great series of books by the late Douglas Adams. The 'trilogy in four parts' as it's sometimes known!). In other words, 'Thanks for all the lovely tax money we've fleeced off you! Now prepare to be right royally friar tucked!' (Rhyming slang! There could be younger readers out there!). And, 'Friar tucked' we *were*!

It simply wasn't *enough* for the people on high, to enforce this *ridiculous* distancing plan! It's incorrectly and inappropriately named in *my* eyes, so it was bound to fly like a concrete pigeon! *That* was the starter for ten! No conferring!

So...let's move on to...*restrictions*!
I suppose we could call them the *little brother* of
the Big Brother, *Lockdown 2020*! Aptly named as
you shall soon see!
Now, the late Sir Terry Pratchett, author of the
excellent Discworld series of books, among others,
used a *brilliant* phrase in one of said books, which I
felt was relevant. 'Authority rarely descends to
street level.'I sense doubt, so I shall explain!
Right, so, referring back to our topic, that of
restrictions, the powerful ones put *plenty* in place!
Basically, anywhere they deemed as 'essential',
read, '*fun*', was closed with immediate effect! Bojo
made his public address, and, by the time the
weekend arrived (convenient, considering a lot of
people *work* during the week, and save the
weekends for some *serious* downtime!) everywhere
was closed! You name it, it was closed! And the
very nature of our lives was transformed overnight!
Quite literally! The schools were closed,
hairdressers,barbers, cafes, cinemas, bowling
alleys, gyms, pubs, restaurants, sporting venues.
They even cancelled seriously big events, like the
Olympics and Wimbledon! Even The Grand
National went virtual, and resembled the kind of
graphics you would normally see in a computer
simulation of a hazard perception test! There were
few exceptions to the rules, painfully few! You
couldn't speak to a GP for a telephone consultation

without getting past a medical receptionist, and giving them *way* too much personal information, before judgement was passed as to whether you were worth a consultation or not! You couldn't(and, still can't, at the time of writing this part, February 2021) access your own dentist, even if you were in so much damn pain you would willingly rip your own head off to ease it! Access to a vet was *impossible*, unless it was an emergency, or to pick up medication for a pet with a chronic ailment! I speak from experience when I say that having two cats both needing annual boosters, was a worrying experience! However, they both needed to see the vet for other matters during that initial lockdown. One had a corneal ulcer, and the other somehow managed to sting her throat! Not at the same time! So, as my local practice had been closed down, due to the pandemic, I was out a small fortune in taxi fares getting them to the only surgery in the chain that was open. It's not accessible by public transport, and that would be the *last* mode of transport you'd consider with an anxious cat in a cat carrier! For the fur baby with the ulcer, this incurred several trips, and as I don't drive, so, I don't have a car, like a naughty schoolgirl I was made to wait outside, in *all* weathers, because, thanks to the government's championing of, 'Outdoors *good*, indoors *bad*', (which sounds strangely reminiscent of Orwell's *Animal Farm*, ' four legs *good*, two legs *bad*.'tenet!), nobody was allowed into the surgery, even though they had perspex screens up! We anxious, worried, concerned pet owners just hung around the car park while our beloved pets were whisked away from us! We weren't even allowed in with them! It has to be one of *the* most surreal experiences of my life to date, when it's bucketing with rain, and you're standing in a car park, while one of the staff are taking payment from you with a wireless card reading machine! *That* actually happened!

So, you can imagine the chaos *this* demonising of indoors caused!

Weddings were cancelled, milestone occasions, special indoor events put on hold, indefinitely, and, at *this* time (February 2021), I still don't believe indoors will *ever* be a reality! Not by a long chalk! So, again, I went a little off topic!

Coming back around to Pratchett's stunning observation, the kicker was, that the people from on high were issuing restrictions left, right, and centre, but, and here's the *important* thing to remember...*they weren't the ones who had to enforce said rules*, she said, in a tone not much above a whisper! *Now* do you see what I mean?

So, while they were all about orderly queues outside shops, social distancing inside *and*, bizarrely, *outside*, only going out for one hour a day, and, later, compulsory mask wearing in shops, indoor spaces and public transport, they weren't the ones on the front line actually having to deal with the general public, and, from experience, there are a *lot* of maladjusted whackadoodles out there, who will go off like two bob rockets if they thought you were looking at them in a funny way! (funny peculiar, not funny ha ha!), so, can you *imagine* what it would be *like* if some poor shop worker were trying to enforce what later became *law* re mask wearing, to such an individual? They could end up getting a lot of verbal abuse, or worse, and that's more than anybody's job is worth! But those government ministers in their ivory towers, just don't *get* what it's like on the ground, having to enforce these rules that *so* many are not happy about! It's not exactly Mardi Gras for any of us at the moment, and we're living our lives through the utterly bo-ring coronavirus updates our First Minister (in my neck of the woods) seems to revel in! I gave up on them a *long* time ago! I'll only be interested once there's a *huge* billboard campaign, dancing girls, big band in the street, playing a standard on loop, entitled, *Everything's Back To Normal Now!* Until that happens, I'm not tuning in! Just tuning out for now!

Continuing with our, 'outdoors *good*, indoors *bad*' theme, it's one thing to get all hoity toity about where you can go in terms of *public* spaces, it's a whole other act to try and dictate to *me*, or anybody *else* for *that* matter, what I can do, what *we* can do, *in our own homes*. Did you get that, government people? *That's* when I realised that we were no longer living in a democratic society, but a *dictatorship*! My home is *my* space, and I feel that crosses a line, when you actually try to tell *me* who I can, or can't invite, into, let me reiterate this, as it's a very important point, *my own home*, and, quite frankly, it's a sacrilege, to even *think* about venturing into that territory, and to try it on, en masse! Let me make this crystal clear...unless the government or the First Minister is, in *any measurable way, paying my mortgage, then they have absolutely no right to tell me what to do in my own home!* And I am fairly certain that I am echoing the sentiments of everybody else who feels that this is taking things *too* far! They really haven't got a case here, and it angers me no end that the police are being called out to places where there'sonly a few people just chatting with friends they haven't seen in a long time, having a drink or two, only to get arrested and issued fines! God! Don't the police have *much* more pressing problems to deal with, say, for example, catching *real* criminals? Or, has it just become the way that *normality* is turning out to be the most heinous crime of all these days...?

So, let us move on to the reaction of the GBP (Great British Public).

When the lockdown was first announced, nobody knew what to expect. Some probably thought it was an excellent opportunity to start learning that new skill, take up that new hobby, learn that new language they'd been meaning to, but kept putting it off. Others thought it would mean more family time, a chance to reconnect with their loved ones. Maybe some even viewed it as a challenge to be met and mastered. What it did come down to, eventually, was that there would be a *lot* of people out there, with a lot of time on their hands. The question was...what would they *do* with it? Two things came to mind for me, t'internet, and...*Netflix!* It's actually no surprise at all that *Netflix* subscriptions went up during lockdown! Well, what *else* could the nation do all day, when they had nowhere to go? The only other service available to them, if you could call it that, were takeaways! The deadly double! Takeaways and *Netflix* subscriptions! Is it any wonder, then, that health issues ensued as the Lockdown went from mere weeks, to *months* of being shut indoors with nowhere to go? This was probably the only scenario where the government would *happily* reverse their much hackneyed tenet of, 'outdoors *good*, indoors *bad*.'

Or...*would* they?

All I can say is, before I continue, is...some people
are *never* happy!
Seems that the people who are *never* happy fall into
two groups. *Narcissists* and *Politicians!*
Maybe they are one and the same! (just my little
joke!).
So...*here's* the thing!
Perhaps they *shouldn't* have made this philosophy
quite as wide ranging as they actually *did*!
And...this would be down to the unfortunate fact
that *some* groups of people *have* to be out and
about in society, otherwise, it would completely
collapse! There is absolutely *no* escaping that fact!
Now, I did refer to, earlier, the 'key' worker, or,
'critical' worker, or, 'essential' worker! All
soubriquets aimed at the poor sods in professions
that were either at the *top* of the pay scale, or, way
down *low*! We're talking minimum wage, those of
us employed by bosses with the mindset of, ' if it
weren't for the unavoidable circumstance that, by
law, I *have* to pay you even *that* much money to do
demeaning jobs for me, then, trust me, I
would!' Welcome to the wonderful world of
Capitalism! Just to clarify, it bothers me *no* end,
that minimum wage earners are tarred with the
same brush, that people make erroneous
assumptions that these jobs are low skilled! In
some cases...they *aren't*! It's all been a mere matter
of the *legal* amount an employer is obliged to pay

you, and what they get you to *do* for it! For the
record, I currently work in pharmacy, dealing with
medication, people, I also have a *certificate,*
(licenced for pills! Little 007 joke there!) and, no
word of a lie, in some supermarkets, there are staff
getting paid significantly *more* than me to scan
shopping! For the record, I am a minimum wage
shill! Setting a legal limit has left the door open to
allow capitalist employers to, almost overnight,
redefine, and reinterpret, our job titles, so, there are
a *lot* of qualified people out there, being paid a *lot*
less than their previous market value! There's also
the added bonus that, minimum wage employers
are not keen, by any stretch of the imagination, to
see their staff progress in any way, via training and
development, because that would mean having to
pay them even *more*! It doesn't mean you are
unsuccessful, if you are in a minimum wage gig!
Far from it! Circumstances dictate in a lot of cases,
and, if you have bills to pay, and you need to eat,
then, it's the best worst choice, right?
Therefore, wasn't it a turn up for the books that,
suddenly, the least respected and valued workers in
society, were given something of an
unexpected...*psychological* boost?
We had gone from being lowly labourers, to super
important people! Flinging such ego boosting
words around with gay abandon, such as,
'essential', 'critical', 'key', in relation to our

insignificant, dead end, 'low to no progression', roles, was intended to incentivise us into keeping the country going, but, it's a great pity such gratitude and thanks wasn't reflected in our pay packets!

Let me tell you something...want to know what I got as a 'bonus'at Christmas, in 2020? From my employer? £100! That's all, and, seemingly, I was lucky to get it! While other similar businesses were giving out *three* times as much to their staff,(and I haven't been off sick once, and I'm closing in on three years at this firm! Hello capitalism! It's good to see you!), all I repeatedly heard from a work colleague, who is starting a new job in a couple of weeks, and hasn't served even *half* the sentence I have at the business, (tells you everything, right?), was that I was *lucky* to be in a job! Capitalists *love* a bit of melon twisting, and the *classic* tactic, of, 'You're lucky to be in this job!' closely followed by the time honoured phrase of, 'There are lots of people who would gladly do your job!' is just one of their mind games, although, deep down, they would be bricking it if you resigned tomorrow, because they are well aware that they would have to advertise the job at a higher rate of pay, or, just lie, albeit indirectly, to attract new talent.

So, while the nation languished at home, there *were* people out there, keeping things running. Pharmacy workers, supermarket workers, postmen (and women!), delivery drivers, binmen,health care workers, and many, many more, who wouldn't normally get a second look if you passed them in the street. They were the backbone of society. Of course, because they worked in the few areas that people could actually go to, it did put them at significant risk of catching the virus. And, in my area, there were so many people floating about, like spectres, lost souls, that you would *never* know there even *was* a lockdown! But, the government's sentiments were *quite* clear! It's quite all right for the masses to eat, get medication, and go to work, if in a 'key'profession, or they couldn't work from home (well, I *clearly* couldn't! I don't have a dispensary at home, and it wouldn't be legal even if I did!), and, that was it! They drew the Maginot line at that! Fun was (and still is!) officially forbidden! People needing life saving treatment had to take a back seat to this exiguous virus! Even *now*, almost a *year* later, nobody knows what's going on! Even the little pleasures in life were taken from us! Remember the days when you felt blue, and a trip to the hairdresser's would give you a boost? Or even meeting a friend you hadn't seen in a while for a trip round town and a coffee afterwards! And, our survey *said*, 'X'(Family Fortunes reference here! I can't do the sound!) to *that*! Yup, fun was indeed, forbidden! We all need the little pleasures in life to get us through

something as massive as a pandemic, FFS!
(younger readers, remember?). But, they just don't
get it! To be honest, they *never* did!
So, we trundled, and continue to trundle on! Like I
said, I refuse to tune into those demeaning televised
updates! It's like watching a Chekhov play being
played out on stage, day *in*, day *out*, where nothing
happens! That's the hallmark of most of his work,
actually! Some call it *genius*, leading the audience
up the garden path to some kind of denouement
('untying of the knot'is the English translation)
which never comes about, while others just see it as
freaking frustrating! (I'm with the latter, actually!)
I've often likened this to us, the masses, being like
the dog tied up outside the supermarket, waiting on
its owner to appear! We wag the tail, hoping to
hear that we can start doing 'normal'again, only to
have our hopes dashed, *again*! Like, when the dog
realises it's *not* their owner who has just appeared,
and they got all waggy tailed for nothing! That's
what it's been like!
And *then*...a ray of sunshine, quite literally!
Or...*was* it?

Madness,Madness, We Call It Madness

Now,the *real* kicker in all this, was, throughout *this*
lockdown, every bank holiday weekend yielded
gorgeous weather!

Easter, the two May bank holidays, and, the regional ones! (local, you get my meaning!). But, as sure as *night* follows *day*, the government were keen to put a spanner in the works! I mean, it's an over zealous, controlling, ' we screwed up *big time* but putting the blame on *you*!' government's worst nightmare for great weather to appear on public holidays, right? When they are trying to encourage people to stay home, but, by the same token, championing that it's safer to be outdoors, they are *still* insistent on us *not* going out! Pick a lane, guys! What I truly resent, about all this, is that *we* were merely reacting *normally* to *abnormal* circumstances! I mean, expecting people *not* to hit the beach and local beauty spots, on a public holiday, when the sun is splitting the rocks, is like going out in the rain and hoping that you won't get wet! See what I mean?

So, while it *wasn't* against the rules to, hit the beach, as so many of us did at that time, given the gorgeous weather, that was a given, they went down the begging road of, 'We know you can do it but we'd much rather you didn't!' to confer compliance.

Then, once they started getting the police to patrol the beaches, one of the few places where ahem, *antisocial* distancing could be practised, people started getting creative!

Considering that indoor gatherings were abolished during lockdown, the great weather did make it easier for people to hold barbecues! And you truly have *no* idea just how irritating some of your neighbours can actually *be*, until you're stuck indoors alongside them twenty four seven, and most of the neighbours in my block were stay at homers! Getting paid to stay in, while I was getting paid *shit* (sorry!) to go out and risk catching Covid! And, as if *that* wasn't bad enough, the *one* friend we had, the last vestige of a vastly shrinking sense of normality, *television*, to offer up a *little* distraction in this time, to help get us through, was being used as a means of overt propaganda against us, serving as a constant reminder that there was a *pandemic*! Seriously, though, did we really *need* reminding of the horror? Orwell would have been saying, 'I told you so!' were he alive today! He saw it coming! Maybe his predictions, re timing, were a *bit* out, but still, *here* we are!

So, how was such an innovative invention deployed in this fashion?

(Come closer, and I'll *tell* you!)

Subliminal advertising!

Yes, you may gasp, people, but, *that* was *my* take on the horror that was unfolding in front of me!

And, horror, it was!

At *this* point, I would strongly suggest, if you haven't already done so, that you read *A Clockwork*

Orange, or, if you aren't currently up for learning a new language (because, said book is written in a sort of 'street speak', language tailor made to be used between close knit groups and gangs, like a code, of sorts. 'Droogs' means 'friends', for example. Been a while since I read it!), get yourself a copy of the film on dvd. I don't want to spoil things for you, but what happens to Alex in that book/film, is *identical* to what was being broadcast by the government! Brainwashing!

So, the concept of subliminal advertising, or selling, was to use commercials to convince potential consumers to purchase products they didn't necessarily need. Fair play, that's the general motivation of advertising, to create a false need. The consumer takes it or leaves it, it's their decision, done deal!

Subliminal advertising, on the *other* hand, is, in essence, advertising, but, with a little something extra thrown into the mix, and *that* would be to *guarantee* that a consumer *will* stump up for your product! No questions asked! 'money out of pocket, I am having some of *that*!'

Like, in the cinema (remember them? People used to sit in halls and watch films! Ah, the good old days!), they used to pump the tantalising aroma of popcorn into the building, so that, even if you didn't *want* popcorn, you soon would! It was later *banned*, because, some people's minds are more susceptible to such things than others!

Case in point...does anybody out there remember that bizarre experiment that Derren Brown guy did, about making people unable to get up off their sofas, a *long* time ago? Yeah, I find it hard not to get up off my sofa at times, but, that's down to the fact that I can't be bothered! There were people reporting that they couldn't get up off their sofas, while others still could, so, there you go!

However...what if the motivation of the advertising wasn't to convince you to sign up for a product, but to *control* your actions?

And *that's* what the government's public information films are all about! Population control! Obeying orders! I mean, Whisky,Tango, Alpha,Foxtrot? (Bit of cool educational code for you all out there! NATO Phonetic alphabet o'clock!).

If I may digress, *ever* so slightly, and get a rewind back to the 1970s, when the Central Office of Information used to broadcast public information films, *Charley Says* (if you are a bit of a super geek, there is a double dvd compilation available,of the same name, on the Network label, containing the best of all of these films!) and all that! Seems even back *then* the government thought we were all idiots who didn't know the dangers inherent in society, and couldn't look after ourselves without a daily dose of being treated like mentally deficient kids who couldn't be trusted to set foot outside the house most days! Victor Lewis Smith does a *brilliant* send up of them on Youtube! Worth scoping out!

The thing is, though, where the current brainwashing films, pop ups, adverts, call them what you *will*, and their 1970s predecessors part company, is in their *approach* to the danger of a given situation.

Now, the 1970s public information films, while hard hitting and demonstrative of what *could* happen, should you not take the advice on offer as to how you should avoid a dangerous situation, (like, no throwing frisbees into power stations and, heaven for fend, actually try and retrieve it, or acting like Willy Weasel instead of behaving like good little Tufty when crossing the road to the ice cream van with his Mum), the current films are, well...patronising, and dictatorial!

That's right! I *said* it!

Generally, they are all made up of little animations that they clearly got some five year olds to do (before all the educational institutions were closed down), with *super* simple statements, like, 'Stay home', 'Book a test', ' You must self isolate,'and so on. See the common denominator in the language? Statements, not requests! Bearing in mind that the government are actually asking the general public to potentially surrender their common freedoms, and that's a *big* ask, you'd expect them to have some *manners*, considering that it was *their* refusal to put the money where it was *supposed* to go, and, by extension, as observed by others I know, they locked down too late, that we are where we are! Oh, but you try telling *them* that! They'll deny the charges, and make the public the villains of the piece, and, given the new, inane Covid legislation that was rushed through parliament, I'd say they worked pretty damn fast to ensure that *we* were *punished* because *they* got *complacent*! No two ways about *that*! They basically thought they could get away with putting a few slates on the roof of the building that we shall call the NHS...and now the roof has caved in, and fallen into a few floors as well! And all because they didn't want to spend a *little* bit extra, to offset a bigger problem! That's my take on visiting medical professionals! Fear shouldn't get in the way, because, if you consult with them early enough, they can do more for you, and if the government had just progressively spent a bit more, instead of backing out altogether, for *years*, then we could have faced this pandemic head on. As a result, I bet you even *more* money has been shelled out, as opposed to what it *would* have cost them, had they been just a *little* more consistent with the cash! As my Mum used to say, 'The deed is done, what do you do with the dagger?'

Returning to our subject, that of *films*, some of them were just, well, seriously *bizarre*! I can talk you through some! Feel free to suspend disbelief! (You might just have to!)

First up, the NHS advert dictating to people that they needed to lose those lockdown pounds! 'Fight Covid 19!' it proclaimed! 'Protect the NHS!' (bit rich coming from the people who underfunded it, and will continue to do so, until they find a good reason to dismantle it altogether!). It featured a fair few overweight people, some with prosthetic limbs, engaged in the battle to lose weight, while some booming, commanding voice over artist got all political with our old friend, the short, sharp, scary statements! No 'please', 'thank you', or even a *hint* of 'appreciation'. From the off, a truly insulting advert, telling people to get off their asses, that they were a bunch of fatties lazing around at home all day, while tactfully glossing over the fact that, under *ordinary*, everyday circumstances, they wouldn't *be* in that situation, but, if all you have available to you is *Netflix* and takeaways, along with extremely limited areas to exercise, what the bloody *hell* did you expect to happen! That people would *miraculously* lose weight? Deluded, that's what it is! Bit of guilt shifting too! The government, far rather than address the fallout of their, cough, cough, *restrictions*, and fully acknowledge that this *would* happen, thought it much more fun to psychologically trick us into being model citizens, despite reacting *normally* to an abnormal situation! 'Oh, so we closed your workplaces, all leisure and fitness venues, but we want you to be okay with that, and be good little boys and girls and be good and healthy because we don't want to take the fall for the NHS being overrun by obesity related cases, cases that would *never* have existed, had we not screwed up!'Talk about compounding the problem! Too focused on Covid 19 to look at other associated problems their restrictions would cause! Thus putting even *more* pressure on the NHS! You've got to love *that*! Sow the wind, reap the whirlwind!

Funnily enough, this advert was pulled not long after it was broadcast, possibly down to the unfounded assertion that losing weight actually stopped you from getting Covid 19! I sense that they had no real proof that this was true! Although, some months later, a revised version of the advert was released, with a blend of old and new footage, with Blondie's *One Way Or Another* replacing the previous, I really don't have the descriptive skills at my disposal, em, hand clapping, rubbish version of the *excellent* Queen song, *We Will Rock You*, only, with the hand clapping in it, and all the good stuff removed from it! Let's go with *that*! You'll know it when you hear it!

Another advert that *really* ground my gears, was the one I call the guilt tripper! This came about when lockdown was lifted, sort of, and we were introduced to the *wonderful* world of 'tiers' And, talk about hitting a fly with a baseball bat, in my area, it was a *five* tier system! I'll come to *that* in a bit!

So, *this* mini marvel featured a business owner being followed by a camera, to her work, talking about how people weren't meant to look for loopholes in the tier system, reinterpret the rules, that you couldn't 'tweet' them, or something! It was like a guilt tripping monologue, and it finished up with her outside her business, saying her business couldn't stay open if people didn't follow the rules! Now, *this* is interesting, because, people, for the most part, *were* following the rules, but, bearing in mind that a cafe comes under *hospitality*, and the fact that, since November 2020 (depending on the area), to *now*, (February 2021), also with rumours abound that some areas of hospitality may not get to trade till *Easter*, it all seemed like something of a pointless venture! Guilt tripping the public doesn't score points with *me*! And, it's also *very* undignified to extol the virtues of not breaking the rules, especially when it was merely delaying the inevitable! That her cafe would close no matter how many guilt trips she inflicted on us! the poor girl was merely a tool to be manipulated by the government to guarantee compliance among the population! But, seriously, with so few places open, did they honestly think the public would wilfully jeopardise the few pleasures that remained available to them?

While I'm on the subject of the undignified, the latest advert that I thought was *completely* out of order, was the one that I shall refer to as the, 'Puss In Boots from the Shrek films' one!

No mystery *there*! I *think*, from the introduction *alone*, you all know the one I mean!

This one, when I first saw it, possibly towards the end of 2020, featured still shots of patients with Covid 19, in oxygen masks, interspersed with NHS staff in visors, wringing their hands, staring straight at the camera! All with those pleading expressions, a la our aforementioned feline friend, when he begs Shrek to take him on his journey. And, the tag line is, 'Look them in the eyes, and tell them you aren't doing all you can to fight Covid-19.' I uttered many an imprecation when I saw it, because I was so *insulted* by it! Like, *once* again, we were being made out to be the scapegoats here! That kind of behaviour is *solely* narcissistic territory, it's their stock in trade. It should *not* be applied to a crisis, where so many people are either being forced to unfairly shoulder unnecessary, misplaced guilt, or are too frightened to set a toe outdoors! For my own part, I seriously resented the implication that I, in some small way, was being held responsible for all this, because I wasn't staying at home! Let me rephrase that. Like many others in a similar situation, I *couldn't* stay at home! As a critical worker, I was mixing with various households, in an indoor environment *five* days a week! What choice did I have? What choice did anyone in a profession that meant they had to go out have? None! No choice! Which is why I hated that advert so much! I still do! I'm *very* curious to know who actually commissioned these adverts! (I'm not done yet!). Who came up with *that*! Some director with delusions of grandeur that they could be a slightly less edgier Quentin Tarantino or something? Aiming for subtle guilt, instead of cutting off policeman's limbs in true Van Gogh stylee? Not on *my* watch! Besides, getting your message across by *begging*, pleading, is *super* undignified! Looks like this joker went way beyond understanding the brief! He practically *rewrote* it! Moving *on*, let's take a look at another one!

As Winter 2020 was closing in on us, the jolly old government were quoting Shakespeare! ' Now is the Winter of our discontent.'and so on! But, with the clever quotes, came the concerns of colder weather meaning that we would be spending more

time indoors! A perfectly natural occurrence for *us*, but a *headache* for the government!
Enter, the scaremongering indoors commercial! Selling us an even more bizarre concept than ever before!
So, opening shot, we see a man coming in from the shops, and into his house, and Covid germs are depicted as a funny form of green smog! It's all over his hands, the handles of the shopping bags, and, like a good little boy, he washes his hands at the sink, all textbook. But, then Mr Voiceover Man appears on the scene, insisting that, even though it's practically *baltic* outside, that we should *open* a window, to let the Covid germs out! I *hate* to point this up, but, we haven't been allowed inside each other's homes for long enough, so it's only going to be people you've been interacting with for months that you'll be sharing the house with! Furthermore, if it's cold outside, and I'm the one forking out for the fuel bills, if I want my window to stay shut, you bet your ass it's staying shut, and *no* pedantic voiceover artist is in a position to tell me, or anyone else, otherwise! Capisce?
The *last* one I shall mention, is the *Sesame Street* one, as it is truly reminiscent of said show, and seeing it repeatedly on T.V. is turning me into Oscar The Grouch!
Otherwise known as *F.A.C.T.S*, a fun acronym (not!) reminding us of the rules we need to follow

to be good little members of society, it's as fellow Scot Sir Billy Connolly said, in *An Audience With Billy Connolly*, one of his landmark gigs, circa 1985, that, to quote him directly, 'Television treats you like you're five years of age,'before he does a *fantastically* funny monologue about the weather! And, *this* advert is *no* exception!

Instead of drawing it all out in a bizarre nursery rhyme, could they not have saved a bit of money on actors, by bringing in our old friend, Mr Voiceover Man, and get him to tell us to, generally, wash your hands, keep your distance, and, where possible, just avoid people altogether! Saves a bit of time, as opposed to talking down to us, and giving us way too much information to remember! Even *now*, I still can't remember what all the letters stand for! God knows what the pensioners out there must be thinking! Did the government honestly think people got *that* far along the road of life if they really needed to be spoken to in that way! Disrespecting your citizens 101! Reddit has a forum that's called *ELI5*, which stands for, ' Explain Like I'm Five.'But, those who post on said forum are actually *giving* fellow Redditors (for that is what they are!) permission to oversimplify concepts that they can't get their heads round! and therein lies the difference! I didn't get the memo in which I gave express permission to be treated like a child!

And that's *exactly* what that abomination of an advertising acronym does! I rest my case!

On an apposite matter, that of being treated like you're *five*, there was one *other* advertising campaign doing the rounds on T.V, which was solely aimed at people with mental illnesses, who were, understandably, finding things *really* hard going. This campaign had to have been the most insulting of them all! As per, there were rinky dinky little cartoons, which looked like some nursery school kid had got the fuzzy felt out, and made animations out of cut out shapes! But...here's the thing! (And, you all knew there would be one, didn't you?), the person doing the voiceovers for them sounded like *she* was five as well! Talking down to these poor people, about how they should be making the best of a bad situation that they *didn't* ask to be in, in the *first* place! With all this talk of ' Candle light teas', (What, are we all being like Hyacinth Bucket/Bouquet, now?) and enjoying being out in the garden, read, ' enjoy your house arrest, and be *thankful* and appreciative for your enforced imprisonment and isolation, and thank the *government*, who made it all possible!'I am *seriously* beginning to wonder what is up with people! What we'd *really* like to do, is start living life again, and not this shoddy, two bit, half life we've all been living of late, under the watchful eye of the nanny state!

I have a serious hatred of gaslighting and psychological brainwashing, and I feel that the government have *really* been working at trying to convince us that, limited social freedoms is really a very good thing! Answer me this...who *for*, exactly? Certainly not the minions enslaved to capitalist employers, earning *just* enough to *survive*, not *live*! We need a little something to keep us going!

Even *more* insulting, is that, at the time of writing this, (February 2021) our First Minister is *super* keen to get the kids back to school...but *refuses* to open any more places to us! The current estimate is, possibly, *March* 2021, when we might be able to get haircuts again, go shopping in town, or grab a half decent mocha! Yup! Keep working you little worker drones, and, if you're *very* good, you *might* get to see the inside of a department store at *some* point this year! It's ludicrous, when you think of all the expense business owners went to, forking out for safety measures, in order to enable them to trade again, and that *still* wasn't enough! The First Minister *still* closed everything down! And, never *once* did she ever mention reimbursing any of those business owners! Even Bojo's attitude is like that of a shop owner! Citing, 'opening up the economy,' like he was a shopkeeper just back his holidays! Madness doesn't even *begin* to describe it!

Now, we knew that lockdown couldn't go on *forever*, and that it was in no way a viable solution to the prevailing problem, right? And, sure enough...it *didn't*, although, for most of us, it certainly *felt* as if it did!

It was like living in a perpetual *nightmare*, the endless little adverts constantly reminding us about it, shops all marked out like something off *The Krypton Factor*, but there weren't any trophies or titles on offer to those of us who managed to successfully partake in the shopping event of the lockdown olympics! It's no fun by any stretch of the imagination, to do the antisocial distancing thing, queuing up for ages! It's also a bit...*soviet* for me!

But, fear not! The government was already rooting around in its little bag of tricks, to inflict even *more* misery on the masses! They were on it like a car bonnet!

I mentioned earlier on, that face masks was compulsory (as in, by law) in enclosed spaces...but, it *wasn't* in the beginning of the pandemic. At the start, it was *optional*, until the government got on its high horse of several hands high, and, in their infinite wisdom, made it an absolute *must*! As well as *this* little doozy, which has become a *major* pain in the ass for me, as I wear glasses, they were kicking about all sorts of thematic buzzwords, to make it look as if they were *actually* doing something about getting society moving again, post lockdown. Such as, 'Road map,'and, 'Traffic Light System', to cite a couple. However, where *I* am, they settled on the, ever so dainty, 'Tier System.'Like we didn't already have too much to remember as it was, now we had even *more* data to process! How mind boggling is *this*? The 'tier'system, (appropriately named, because it caused us to cry tears of *frustration* at the sheer, inane nature of it!), was laid out on, I am *not* kidding, *five* levels! (I told you I'd go into this in a *little* more detail, didn't I?). I can't remember *all* the minutiae, because it's so bloody *boring,* but, the idea behind it was that, tier zero was classed as, ' as close to the normality that we once knew and loved,'to tier five, which is, 'total lockdown'Tiers one through four, (or, 'protection levels'as they are sometimes referred to, *what* a joke! Since *when* was closing everything fun to the public ever classed as 'protecting'them? I may have an Honours Degree in English, but I reckon *any* individual would have as big a problem with *that* definition as I do!) are all, 'some places are open, some are not'and a whole load of minutiae in between! *Still* too confusing! Whoever has been tasked that assignment, with naming all of these measures, must be some sort of fantasy sci fi writer! Did they exhume and reanimate the corpse of Philip K Dick? (The 'K'stands for 'Kindred'fact fans! Just in case you were wondering!). You wouldn't get that kind of warped redefining of what is *super* obvious to the *rest* of us, any other way! Then again, Monsieur Dick was out of his head on prescription medications a lot of the time, so I suppose he has an excuse! For Heaven's sake! It's not like a blind man running for a bus wouldn't notice! Call these things by their right and proper names! Take a leaf out of Confucius's book! He said, ' The beginning of wisdom is to call things by their proper name.'Wise words from a wise man...and this *not* 'calling things by their proper name.'activity, that the government are super mad keen on, tells you a *lot*, doesn't it? Not getting to do anything *normal* is a *restriction*! Capisce? Honestly, if everyone went around renaming and redefining clear cut concepts, the world would be in an even *worse* state than it is now! Can you imagine the chaos? 'I'm off to clear some snow with my shovel.''That's not a shovel, it's a metal scoop!'your friend might say! All the same, but *different*!

And so it came to pass, that tears, sorry, *tiers*, were very much in evidence! I do have truck with a tier numbered *zero*! Zero, is, well, *zero*! As in, *nothing* at all! If you get a blood test, and there is *zero* presence of a substance, then, it doesn't count, or register! Crazy from the get go, right? Just some bullshit reason to differentiate us from the rest of the U.K! 'Oh, so you have *three* tiers? I will *see* your three tiers, and *raise* you two more!' *Completely* insane!

Of course, everything brings its own problems, and it wasn't too long before there were posts popping up on Facebook community groups imploring fellow citizens to follow the rules, for fear of being downgraded to a different tier! Given that my location is quite densely populated, we were doing *very* well indeed to remain in the 'magic number' zone! (as in, ' three is the magic number.' Cue for a song!). Nobody wanted to venture into tier four territory, as *that* was but a few steps shy of tier *five*! The dreaded *lockdown* level! We really wanted to hang on to the pitifully few remaining freedoms the tier system granted us, but, who can tell when there's a virus doing the rounds? People can't afford to stay home with children to feed and bills to pay, and the asymptomatic among the masses didn't even know they had it! At *least*, in tier three, non essential retail could remain open, but, how long would the honeymoon last?

It wasn't long before our First Minister started throwing her toys out of the pram, bleating about some rebels travelling between areas that had different tier allocations! To be honest, given the restrictions, there *wasn't* a great deal of difference, if anything, the freedoms differentiating the tier levels were marginal at best. So why she was turning into a spoilt brat about it all was *anybody's* guess! And, it was *her* idea to implement it, although, from what I have observed of late, the First Minister and Bojo tend to play off one another, a bit like two kids sitting next to each other in class, who copy each other's answers! There's just this mad scramble to see who can present their work first, in order to appear like the innovate one in the equation! The person with the genius and creativity (snigger!) to come up with something truly revolutionary! Oh, there'll be something revolutionary in the offing all right, just, *not* quite what they had in mind! Meanwhile, Christmas was looming on the horizon, and, with it, impending Winter nights and more time spent indoors. As the government had been such *wonderful* proponents of the, 'outdoors *good*, indoors *bad*,'principle, this posed a problem! With Christmas fast approaching, and families wanting to spend time with each other at this time of year, having been separated for so long, virus cases would almost certainly reach unprecedented levels, so, what could they *do* about it? What possible *angle* could they use to discourage people from meeting up at Christmas, without coming across as

being completely...*totalitarian* about it? What possible *approach* could they take, to make everyone sit up and listen, convince them that hooking up with their nearest and dearest was a *bad* idea?
The answer may surprise you!

<u>Merry Christmas Everyone!</u>
<u>(Sense The Tone!)</u>

So...in order to arrive at our answer, we have to mention *two* things! Ready for this? Kent, and, September!
Confused? *Don't* be! I am here to help you make sense of this, and other things! You only need to ask!
Right, then, let's get down to the nuts and bolts, shall we?
As I stated earlier, Christmas was fast approaching, and the nation was in thrall, on the edge of their seats, waiting, and wondering, with bated breath, as to whether, after this entire *shitstorm* of the year that was 2020, there might just be the possibility of a, heaven for fend, and saints preserve us, *normal* Christmas!
Okay, peeps, *not* going to lie to you, but, *initially*, it appeared as though getting to spend time with our loved ones during the festive season, was actually going to happen! Despite the cancellations of

numerous lighting up ceremonies across the country, there was always a chance that *some* things might stay the same, pandemic, or *no* pandemic. I'not one for spoilers per se, but, there'a *clue* embedded in my narrative! Have you spotted it yet? If you *have*, then you are one smart cookie, and I have *great* pleasure in awarding you ten points to your team table! As for the rest of you, stay tuned!

So, showing some sort of solidarity, the devolved governments decided to adopt a four nations approach (just to clarify, *nothing* to do with rugby! Neither the *place*, nor the *sport*! Sorry!), and basically sit round a big, geographically as well as socially, distanced table, to thrash out some sort of workable solution for when old St Nicholas was due to pay us a visit. It was finally agreed upon, that there would be a Christmas...*amnesty*, where there would be a week long window stretching from Christmas Eve to New Year's Eve (or, Hogmanay, as it's known in *my* neighbourhood! It's thought to be derived from French , but, that's all I've got on that!), enabling people, for the first time in *long* enough, to actually *see* one another, in the *flesh*, *indoors*, and this amnesty applied right across the board! No geographical borders, barriers, or any other such thing to consider! It was all uniform!

Now, this was all agreed upon at the beginning of December 2020. Cue people fervently trying to get everything arranged for the big day! Travel and accommodation arrangements, food shops bought, pets boarded, the whole box and dice! No mean feat when you don't have a lot of time to get things organised!

So, it was official! The governments were actually going to let us have some modicum of normality! At *long* last! Christmas was *on*!

And, to quote from the *Status Quo* song, *Burning Bridges*, it was 'off again!'How so?

Well...now we come to *Kent*!

And, the *small* matter of a *variant* strain!

This *variant* was first spotted in *Kent*, and said to be much more transmissible that the *original* strain that caused us all to be in lockdown in March 2020. What this *means*, is that it can be passed on human to human, at a *much* faster rate, so, there was a greater likelihood of *more* cases emerging as a result! It was really only a matter of time before mutations started appearing on the radar. To my current knowledge, there's also an *African* one (originating in Rio, the *place*, and *nothing* to do with the woman who 'dances on the sand'in the *D*uran Duran song!) doing the rounds, as well as some exiguous strain located in Bristol! It's *so* hard to keep up! But, I'm doing my best! It *is*, after all, the nature of a virus, to mutate in order to ensure its survival. It's not like it was going to just maintain the same composition throughout! This is why we get colds every year! Viruses *change*, and it's down to our immune systems to combat every subsequent strain! Maybe we should view viral variants as software packages you'd get for a computer system! Covid 1.0! Covid XP! Covid Vista! Covid 7! (you get the idea!). I'm also giving away something of my digital knowledge! Showing my age, right? Not that I *mind*!

I don't suppose I have to slow walk you all to an epiphany, but, you've probably worked it out already!

Christmas was cancelled!

Barely a *week* before the *big* day, they pulled the plug! And everybody had to revise their plans...*again*!

New tier restrictions were put in place, in near enough, the *whole* of England, meaning that nobody could go *anywhere*, without breaking a law, or three, and, in *Scotland*, aka Blighty, the First Minister narrowed down the week long amnesty, to, wait for it...just *one* day! *Christmas Day*! I mean, you *couldn'* t make it up! All travel, the whole shooting gallery, was to be confined to that *one* day, and, as you *know*, nobody *sane* could manage a decent Christmas in just one day! See? Power trippers, the lot of them!

And...before you all come at me, saying, 'How could you *say* such egregious things?'well, I *do* have *one* more thing to mention!
Enter...*September*!
So...*what* if I were to tell you that the governments had been in the know about the, what I shall *now* call, the ' Kent Variant', since that very month? They knew of its existence, and yet, they *still* agreed on the week long amnesty, at the start of December, only to pull it away a week before Christmas! Raises some questions, don't you think? Namely, why agree to a Christmas amnesty at *all* if there was the background threat of a much more contagious strain? Why offer people hope of a *normal* Christmas, only to wheech it away at the very last minute? Seriously, if they'd been closely monitoring it, the *last* thing you'd expect them to do would be to allow people to make plans, especially with so much hanging in the balance!
On an apposite matter, and this was something that just occurred to me the other day, people have *every* right to be browned off, frustrated and annoyed, if they have been put out big style!
Allow me to explain!
If a person is in *their right and proper place at a particular time*, then, they aren't being inconvenienced in any way, so, if you usually go to work on a particular day, work a particular shift on that day, there's no disruption, ergo, no bother!

Whereas, someone who *isn't* in *their right and proper place at a particular time*, is put out! So, all those government ministers making all their rules, all their fine speeches, all of their blah,blah, blahing, is just another day at the office for *them*! Meanwhile, the minions are having to *constantly* adapt to these ever changing rules and restrictions, making plans for Christmas, then, unmaking them, and living very differently to what they are used to! To extend this point further, I recently had an appointment with my GP surgery! Unfortunately, due to the lockdown train schedule, and, generally, this is often the case with public transport, in order to make the appointment, I arrived half an hour early. It was either *that* or be too late, and I did have to go to work afterwards. I should also point out that I had to take the appointment because circumstances dictated that I had to turn up at super silly o'clock!

On arrival, I was standing at the door, (as, due to covid, they don't allow people to use the waiting room) and spoke into the intercom, explaining my situation. I was the *only* person there, and they *wouldn't* let me wait inside! They expected me to walk around in a biting wind, saying I had to come back at my appointed time! I sat outside and read my book for a while! See, everyone in that surgery was *in their right and proper place at a particular time*. They were in the *right* place, at the *right* time!

Meanwhile, my *right and proper place* would have been in my flat, getting ready for work!

Instead, I had to get up *very* early to catch a train that I *knew* would get me in too early, but it was the latest one I could get! I had to miss my breakfast, sit around in the cold for half an hour for a procedure that only took a few minutes, and it was the earliest appointment they had, and the train never turned up, so I had to get the *next* train back, then I had a very rushed breakfast before going to work, and I had to make up almost an hour and a half, spread over two shifts, because, had I tacked it all on to my shift that day, I wouldn't get home, and my lunch, till 3pm! Phew! See what I mean about how downright irritating it is to be put out big time? Everyone expects to be put out a *little* bit, but when the inconveniences and trials just drag on and on, it's no wonder we're all sceptical as to whether the government has a plan to get us out of the pandemic at all, or if they're just making it up as they go along! (Sure looks like it!) It really does get to a point where all the placatory talk, and vague assertions as to when we *might* see *some* sense of normality, just don't carry any weight anymore, and, I'll admit that, whenever a politician opens their mouth, I simply pull a Kylie on them! I sing, 'la la, la la la la la, la la la, la la la la laah.' Not listening! Talk to the *hand*, parliament people!

And, so it came to pass that, as more restrictions were laid upon us, the government sugarcoated the measures with that God awful word...*Safety*! Yes! They were summarily doing away with the last vestiges of human rights, by disallowing Christmas, but trying, albeit *pathetically*, to justify our social imprisonment by claiming that they had our wellbeing at heart! I'll crack the jokes around here! They saw this as an even *bigger* threat to the pitiful NHS resources they had! Basically, the *last* time I checked, catching a virus *wasn't* a criminal offence! We are *human* after all! It's a fact of life! So...*why* do I get the impression that *this* is what's happening *now*? That we've all been branded as potential plague carriers, and *deserve* to be punished! *Bad* little humans! Walking around the planet infecting other humans! Putting pressure on the NHS! No ownership on the lack of funding in *this* equation! Nope! Just offload their shortcomings on to *us*! Give us the round trip on the guilt express! Woo! Woo! (that was the train whistle, in case you were wondering! Not Tourettes!).

So...*once* again, we were like tigers pacing the cage!

Were we *ever* going to see normality *again?*

As 2020 drew to a close, we were convinced that we'd seen the worst of the pandemic.

Or...*had we?*

Now, while all of this mask wearing, social distancing, lockdown ballyhoo was going on, there were some dedicated scientifically minded boffins actually knuckling down to some serious research, in the race to find a vaccine! There was a *lot* at stake! You know what they say about pharmaceuticals! 'Big Pharma, Big Money!'Okay, maybe they don't *actually* say it in the wider world, but, it *is* true, in essence! There's big bucks in the pharmaceutical industry, and if you happen to be the lucky CEO running the company that comes up with the vaccine that could, well, not exactly *save* humanity, but, give it a fighting chance, then, you're on to a winner!

Getting people to *take* it, however, is a *whole* other act!

So, let's take a look at the runners and riders in the Corona Cup Steeplechase!

First up, we have the vaccine representing *Pfizer*! Real big hitters in the pharmaceutical business! They're the guys behind, among other things, *Viagra*! The salvation of inadequate feeling men prone to erectile dysfunction! A very polite, user friendly term that avoids using the *much* more colloquial, 'Can't get it up!'

But, the *kicker* with this one, was its *massive* storage issue!

It had to be stored, in a freezer, at -80 degrees celsius!

Naturally, this was somewhat problematic, but it was the first one out of the gate! And it required so much dry ice that, were it still going today, *Top Of The Pops* would have to cancel their performance schedule for the next *year* at least! And, Heston of Blumenthal, creative chef a go go, would have to hold off making any more of his Willy Wonka inspired creations for a while! *Not* a popular option with the dry ice enthusiasts out there!

Behind door number *two*, we have the *Astra Zenica* aka the 'Oxford' vaccine! No sub zero storage issues with *this* baby! A surefire hit with GP surgeries, vaccination centres, and hospitals up and down the country, for this characteristic *alone*! If memory serves, *Astra Zeneca* are pretty big in the insulin based side of things! They make *Lantus* products, among others. Bit of professional knowledge kicking in!

And, *finally*, the *third* contender in our competition, the *Moderna* vaccine! I have got *nothing* on that one! Maybe it's the dark horse in our steeplechase!

So, given that scientific progress had made such leaps and bounds, maybe *this* was cause for celebration! Freedom at last!

Or...maybe *not*!

As the Winter of our discontent rolled on and on, the powers that be were working on rolling out their vaccination programmes! Their aim, to get the vulnerable exterminated...sorry, *vaccinated*, as quickly as possible! (just my little joke!).

But, what you all have to understand here, is that these 'vaccines' were experimental! From what I can gather, from work colleagues who have received it, the information is that it won't actually prevent you from getting COVID 19, but it will mean getting a milder version of it, should you happen to fall ill with it! That does *not* sound like a 'win' to *me*! No doubt you all have your own views on the vaccines, and you're all perfectly entitled to have them, whether they align with mine, or not. In principle, I think the deal that is being offered here, via the vaccination programme, is that there's no need to, 'fear the reaper', as the song by *The Blue Oyster Cult* suggests, because, getting a milder form means you're less likely to die from it. Think of it like either going to the electric chair, and instant death, or commuting your crimes to a life sentence. One way means immediate death, and closure. The *other* means a longer life, but you're never really *free*! There will always be that nagging doubt every year, as to how mild your illness might get. In subsequent years, the vaccines will be adapted and modified, in accordance with the scientific data, but, well, once you've got on that ride, it's very hard to come off it! In that, when something new comes along, a vaccine is your only hope, and what if it happens again? Will you compromise on your lifestyle because the vaccine hasn't been discovered yet? Just barricade yourself indoors for *another* year, living in fear, because it's been drummed into society at large that the vaccine is the, 'my way or the high way.' option? 2020 was *no* picnic for the people with health conditions who had to shield from the virus! Shut away for months on end! Is that *any* way to live? Vaccines aren't discovered overnight, so, what is one to do in the mean time? I call being solely reliant on vaccines as being the, 'There's an app for that' mindset. This phrase featured in a commercial, as a tag line, a while back, but the nation appears to have taken it to heart, only, supplementing 'app' with 'vaccine'. It is *not* the done thing to be complacent in the face of such matters! Maybe we were fortunate *this* time around, but something *far* deadlier could be waiting to pounce in the future! Just saying!

Anyway, the first in line for this all new experimental therapy (let's call it what it *really* is! Do Confucius *proud*!), were care home residents, their carers, workers in the health sector, and so on!

Then it went down and down, over eightys, over seventys and on it went. The people *way* down the pecking order were the over fiftys, who, at a conservative estimate, *just* might see the syringe in *May*! Looks like we could be in lockdown a *lot* longer than first thought!

And, I have a reason for believing *this* will be the case!

According to reports, even the vaccinated among us are still *carriers*!

Yes, you read that right! So, it makes me wonder just how *long* we have to wait to see our old friend, normality, again!

The government's approach to all this, is to give the vulnerable groups their *first* dose of the vaccine, but, instead of administering the *second* dose in a few weeks, (because most vaccines, or even pretenders to the throne *claiming* to be vaccines, are given via two doses) they are waiting a staggering *twelve* weeks to complete the courses, because, in their infinite wisdom, they want the vulnerable groups to have *some* level of protection, and if that means diluting the supply, and, by extension, limiting the proven efficacy of the treatment, then, be it so! I'm more of a proponent of, get everyone vaccinated in the requisite time, and then GPs won't have the headache of keeping on top of patients they haven't seen in long enough, and a *lot* can happen in three months! Some elderly patients might need reminding, or could forget altogether! I reckon my depopulation/extermination theory is looking pretty good right now! If the vulnerable aren't *fully* protected, then all bets are off as to whether, in spite of receiving their first dose, COVID 19 won't pay them a visit and finish them off! And the government can say that they made an effort to save them, although half assed at best! You *know* that they have to be seen to be actually *doing* something! That's why politicians make such a big deal of photo opportunities! It's their insurance policy! To chronicle that they were *doing* something! For future generations to gaze and gawp at!

It's interesting to note that, while vaccinating the vulnerable was the priority, just to show that they allegedly *care* about the older, more feeble members of society, did it *ever* cross anyone's mind, at all, that a *lot* of these people are, ' economically inactive', according to the ONS? (Office of National Statistics). You would think that the vaccine would be rolled out to *all* critical workers. After all, none of them could stay at home! They, like *me*, had to go out in the name of duty, and had to mix with people in the wider world, so, surely they should have got first dibs, right? *Wrong*! Just as there is a good reason for doing something, there's *always* something sinister, lurking in the background, and it can't be easily dismissed! People focus too much on the, ' no way would a country do *that* to its population!'You think? If circumstances deemed it necessary, it would! And, you can be sure that there would be widespread ad campaigns conditioning and convincing us that euthanising the least productive members of society was, 'right', and, 'fair', ' for the greater good.'I'm not the only person who has made such observations, let alone believed them! Despite the vaccination programme, though, normality seems *quite* a long way off for us all, and, leaving so much time between doses not only harms the patients, but it harms the economy as well, because the restrictions will remain in place. It looks like we are back at square one, especially since, vaccine or *no* vaccine, we *still* have to socially distance, we *still* have to wear masks, we *still* have to live with restrictions, almost a *year* on! And, maybe even longer than *that*!

Here's a little something for you to mull over...I watched a documentary series on Channel 5 recently (don't judge me! I am but a Freeview pleb, but even *this* station produces some quality programming on occasion!), about the bubonic plague. It was in three parts actually, really interesting!

Okay, back to the plot!

So...here's the thing!

According to *this* series (and, it was fascinating to discover that the disease was passed on by body lice, and not rats as first thought), there had been outbreaks of the plague in the past, so people were immune to it, until this *new* strain of plague started killing everyone off. The nobility, and the rich, fled London to escape it, including Charles the Second! However, the plague had gone in *two years*, and that was allowing it to run, unchecked, and they had no vaccines back then! It did kill off a lot of people, but, *why* do I get the feeling that, even with all of our scientific breakthroughs, and technology, that *we* could be looking at the *same* time frame? What is happening? From what I have heard *so* far, Summer holidays abroad are not to be booked, no 'staycations' at Easter (that's holidaying on home turf, if you aren't familiar with the term! 'Hameldaeme' is the Scottish variant of this term!), only a 'phased' reopening of schools, and *no* word on non essential businesses reopening, and, it's just beyond mid February 2021! I'd say that you could say 'sayonara!' to any chance of pubs, cafes and restaurants reopening soon, and even if they *did*, they would have to *drastically* adapt to allow customers in, to the extent of a significant loss of revenue in the process, like they haven't lost enough as it is!

So...*still* sold on the whole concept of the vaccination programme?

So...towards the end of 2020, there was officially a vaccine programme in hand. Things were almost certainly looking up, and we had turned a corner, of sorts, in the battle against COVID 19!

It is, however, time to rewind back to the Christmas Day amnesty!

For one glorious, stress riddled day, the nation could celebrate, albeit with the looming spectre of the government tut tutting even this *one* pitiful concession! We were bound to pay for our gross insubordination, our rebellious attitude, all because we wanted to do something, well...*semi* normal at best! What's more normal than celebrating Christmas? Life is short!

I suppose, at *this* point, it's appropriate to mention the quote from *Romans 6:23*, 'For the wages of sin is death.'

And, even *perceived* sin, read, rebelling against the government (because, I am willing to bet you anything you *like* that they secretly hoped that people wouldn't leave their homes to spend Christmas with their families if they had to fit it all into a tiny twenty four hour window!), would come at a *price*!

Seems that the government work to quite a peculiar rate of exchange! If they were running a *Bureau De*

Change, you'dget a *lot* less bang for your proverbial buck, folks! Remember, kids, the house always wins! I call it,'the Green Zero effect.' As seen on a roulette wheel!
So...for that *one* day of festivities, fun and frolics, that brief, fleeting escape from all the misery of the year, they decided to *punish* us again, citing that this *one* day was the cause of all manner of new cases popping up! Blaming *us*, distracting us, while they deftly swept aside the hoo hah they created over their week long Christmas amnesty and their knowledge of the Kent strain since *September* 2020!
So...it was *Goodbye* Tier *Three*! It was fun, while it lasted!
And... Hello, *Lockdown 2021*!
Basically, we were *back* where we started!
Being treated like children, *again*!
But...*this* time, it was even *worse*!
As things stood with the tier system, we were in level three, as you know, so there were still some of life's little pleasures available to us!
That *is*...until the First Minister decided to go on her, 'I have to be seen to be doing *something*' crusade!
If you thought that there wasn't much *more* misery she could inflict on the population, then you would be *wrong*!
Very...*very* wrong indeed!

I'll give you an example!

Under Tier three restrictions, we could all go *inside* a coffee shop, or cafe, for a coffee, or whatever takeaway snacks took our fancy, from an extremely limited range, provided we observed the, what I call, *antisocial distancing* rules! This was something *Greggs* the bakers did, to the letter! No more than *two* people in the shop at a time, screens, masks, the whole shooting gallery! And, even this made things just a *little* bit easier to bear. After all, what's life without the little things, like, for *me*, a mocha and a gingerbread man from the bakery next to the work? An occasional treat to keep the spirits up!

Well...the First Minister just *had* to go and rain on our parade!

At her *next* 'review' read, 'up the human misery because I'm not prepared to waste my time by keeping things the *same*!' campaign, and, I am *not* kidding, she decided that cafes and takeaway places could only operate, *if they had a hatch*, because, she was *back* to her, 'outdoors *good,* indoors *bad*' routine! So, she'd effectively punted us all back outdoors, in *all* weathers, may I add, (and Blighty doesn't exactly have the *best* reputation for fabulous weather at the best of times!). Bearing in mind that we'd all been queuing up inside the bakers, like *good* little boys and girls, wearing the masks (which I absolutely *hate*! They've caused my nose to run non stop, my glasses to steam up, and I have had *no* end of skin issues because of them!) doing the distancing thing, and that, we were all served quite quickly, so the longest we were actually indoors was less than *five minutes*, I just think she came up with the hatch idea for the hell of it! According to research, in order for the virus to effectively spread, you would have to be in *super* close contact with a carrier for a full on fifteen minutes to stand any chance of catching it! (Not that you would actually set out to do such a thing!).

As a result, places that had no such facilities had to close, and, again, I'm willing to bet you *anything* you *like*, that she *secretly* hoped all of these businesses, who had already shelled out a *lot* of money to make their premises safe, would become disheartened, throw in the towel, and decide that the juice really wasn't worth the squeeze.

However, she didn't bank on the more *creative* business owners!

I'll be awarding *them* some *serious* cool points, as they didn't put serving hatches in, but, *instead*, allowed their customers to place their orders at the *entrance* of the premises, with the customers standing outside, while their food and drink orders were prepared indoors by the staff! Ingenious! And the bonus ball is that our First Minister *can't* sound off or say *anything* about it, because, nobody is waiting *indoors*! They are queuing obediently *outdoors*! That's not against the rules...unless she states, in *no* uncertain terms, that cafes, coffee shops and takeaways *must* close their doors, *no* exceptions! I speak from my own observations, because I have seen a few places of the genre adopt this very approach, that of taking orders at the door. I am totally with them on this one, because, as previously mentioned, the First Minister screwed these businesses over the *first* time around, getting them to meet covid safe criteria, only to do a complete 360 , and say it wasn't good enough! She did the same to the pubs as well! So, getting around *ridiculously* stringent rules with a *little* bit of ingenuity gets a well deserved hat tip from *me*! Another part of the surprise package, that is the *Lockdown 2021* strategy, was that, while it was already *bad* enough that you had to go *outside* to meet up with your relatives, (weather permitting, I mean, who wants to meet up in a *hurricane*?), they really worked at cracking down on *that* too! How? By reducing the number of people you could meet up with, yes, even *outdoors*! *Now*, you were only allowed to meet up with *one* person from another household, for your daily one hour of exercise! (Because, they still want *some* of us to be sane enough to go back to normality when this *nightmare* eventually comes to an end!) Cue the streets and parks being *rammed*, packed to the rafters with bored, angry, frustrated people, just going to the few places left available to them, that wouldn't involve incurring a fine of some description! Or a police caution!

For my part, as there aren't any decent parks in my area, and I am constantly out and about because of my lowly, critical, key worker job, I am forever seeing these little groups, trying to hold things together by holding on to the very last vestiges of a sense of normality that is becoming frayed around the edges. As I love to give people, and things suitable soubriquets, I dubbed these groups as, if there were *two* parties, *Pandemic Pairs*, and, family groups came under the *Pandemic Posse* category! Things should be called by their right and proper name, after all, and, it's because of the pandemic, and the incumbent restrictions, that this dynamic has become a part of our everyday lives. It'll catch on, *trust* me!

So...as we are *still* in Lockdown as things *currently* stand, (although, at the time of writing this, February 2021, there's to be a phased opening of the schools next week. Good luck with *that* First Minister!) which, to me, is a bit *mad,* as there's a vaccination programme in place, and we really need to look to the future, and what that might possibly entail. It is, understandably, something of a hot topic on these shores, so, just *how*, exactly, are we going to get *out* of it?

... with bored, angry, frustrated people, and
some ... ... to them that
would ... ... of some
description. Dr.s police caution.

The Slow Walk To Freedom
(Or...The Road To Hell?)

Now we come to the nuts and bolts! The way out!
Exit stage left!
So, the powers that be are determined to look at
'data'not 'dates'when it comes to deciding how we
ease ourselves out of this mess!
In March 2020, we were all but plunged into this
crisis, without asking for it! Nobody asks for *this*!
I'm curious as to whether we really ever *will* be
able to live freely after all this. I read online that
our First Minister has more or less already decided
that, irrespective of how successful the vaccination
programme proves to be, the country will still be
placed in *another* lockdown, next Winter, if
restrictions are lifted too soon! And, just *how* soon
is *too* soon? Our hard fought social freedoms can't
be restored to us soon enough! Or has this
pandemic given our governments *carte blanche* to
issue lockdowns at will, whenever the mood takes
them? I have *long* suspected that the concept of,
what I call, 'rolling lockdowns'will feature *very*
strongly in our futures for years to come! They
might even be an annual gig, contingent upon the
receipt of favourable, or, unfavourable data! This
presents the *perfect* opportunity for the *continual*
underfunding of the NHS. Think of *all* the money

and resources they could get away with providing, if they made social restrictions *seasonal*, to the point where they would be, albeit *reluctantly*, adhered to! The flu season would be the one to watch! And doesn't this tie in nicely with the First Minister's threat of a lockdown next Winter? It's a thought, right? And, no coincidence! There's also the *very* strong possibility that the mask wearing and social/antisocial distancing measures will be in evidence, at least for the coming *year*! Are there to be *no* pleasures *left*? Or is the plan to *progressively* dismantle society, using the pandemic as ground zero. as a means to *completely* rewrite normality? To wilfully reconfigure and warp normality to the point that distancing, isolation, distrust of other fellow humans will be the accepted norm in years to come? What I'm trying to express here, and it's a *big* fear of mine, is that, should these measures continue for much longer, will we *forget* what *normality* is? Or, was? It's so difficult trying to uphold one's traditional social values when there are opposing forces coming at you from all sides, dominating your every waking moment, encouraging you, strong arming you into accepting a *new normal*, one that you decidedly do *not* want to adopt! I think the time has come to hold the frame, people! Keep the *true* normality flag flying! Act like a courtier, but be forever waiting for that day, when you can go to concerts, pubs, restaurants, gyms, *anywhere* in the wider world, *mask free*, and be finally *free*! (Maybe I should wake up!)

I have to admit that, in the face of Lockdown(s) there are some people out there pushing the envelope, engaging in what I refer to as, ' acts of minor rebellion.'In saying this, I mean that, while there are so few places for people to go at the moment, I have great respect for those of you out there, who are taking the minor freedoms that remain, and really having a go at making them work for you! So, the gyms are closed, but there are gym bunnies out there in need of an exercise fix, so, what do they do? Take to the streets, in *all* weathers! Rain, snow, the works! In a gym, the weather isn't an issue, but outdoors can have a great deal of bearing on whether a gym bunny gets their exercise that day, so the weather doesn't put them off. *That's* how you get round a restriction, you find another way!

It's also pie in the sky to think that, Bojo the clown stated, in an online report, that *this* would be the *last* lockdown! Oh, and does he bloody *think* so? If, as *he* and our First Minister claims, that 'data'not 'dates'will be their guide to getting us out of Lockdown 2021, It doesn't take a genius to work out that, as a result of us all being cooped up for three months solid (could be longer, not sure yet!), once the non essential retail becomes available to the masses, there will be a social *stampede* as we all try to spend the vouchers we got for Christmas, get to the hairdresser for a much needed haircut, grab a piece of this rare glimpse of normality, generally get our affairs in order, before another Lockdown looms! And, there *will* be another one! Case numbers will soar, because, there is absolutely *no* way in *hell* that the government will be able to present an argument persuasive enough to get people to stay at home once all the shops reopen! They would be on a hiding to nothing, because, that's all they've been doing for the past three months! (regions may vary!).

So, while they are all currently congratulating themselves on the driving down of cases, because, it's *all* about the numbers, not the human misery, they are missing one little detail. It's down to the immobilising of the public, that this has occurred! They are failing to look at it in *real* time, under realistic conditions! Couldn't they have done a contrast and compare? Found a fine balance between fairly functioning society levels, to total lockdown scenario, and maybe, just, *maybe* found a level they were willing to accept? Cases versus how much of the economy could remain active, instead of all this to-ing and fro-ing! That's *not* progress! Didn't Einstein say something about insanity being about doing the *same* thing, but expecting *different* results? That's what *this* is! 'Oh dear, cases are *up*, lock the country down!' 'Cases are *down*, whoopee! Time to lift some restrictions!' 'Oh, cases are *up* again, because people have been going stir crazy at being shut indoors for months and are actually going out! Let's lockdown again!' That sounds like a thematic version of the song by *The Average White Band*! 'Let's go round again...'

And, on it goes! Is it any wonder we're in this perpetual holding pattern, with such backward thinking being proposed by the people in power? As we are in something of a no man's land situation, then, our rationale must reflect that! We don't know what we're dealing with, so it stands to reason that a more... *experimental* approach is the way out! No hitting a fly with a baseball bat, but more, graphic equalising, or, when you're getting something made bespoke. A minor adjustment here and there, and there should be some progress. If you stumble across something that *works*...build on it, see where it takes you!

Staying with the subject of backwards thinking, let us face north!

To *my* territory!

So, while Bojo soujourns in lala land about his hopes for this being his *last* lockdown, (really, *not* happening!), the First Minister is entertaining something *equally* as unrealistic and inane!

Standby...this is *good*!

Right, so, while *some* of us believe that Covid 19 won't be disappearing any time soon, and may just, in fact, end up being just another irksome illness to dodge as part of our everyday lives, like the cold, the First Minister reckons it can be completely *eradicated* from our shores! I can hear you all laughing from here! Show of hands as to how many of you out there reckon *that's* never going to happen! Let me *see* now...yup, *quite* a few! Good to know I'm not alone!

Even though her scientific advisors have stated that eradication isn't possible, she's still hanging on to this belief. And such a hard lined approach is *bound* to have consequences for the rest of us. When some people get an idea into their heads, they can be like dogs with bones, determinedly, doggedly persevering in the face of adversity, before realising that they are beaten!

Meanwhile, as they disappear like wraiths, with a lovely pension to feather their nests when their plan becomes a *fiasco*, it's the public who are left with the legacy of their lunacy, and someone *else* has to restore order from the chaos! What kind of leadership example is that? To summarily screw over society, then be *rewarded* with a pension that would make anyone of my minimum wage standing, *salivate*!

Essentially, the solution to getting us out of lockdown is *not*, more lockdowns! Anyone with *half* a brain could tell you *that*!

The Nostradamus Effect

Okay, I'm going to venture into the world of the unknown!
Let's talk, *predictions*!
Just like our friend, Nostradamus!
He was something of a go to guy on that sort of thing!
At the time of writing this, as previously mentioned, in my area, so far, there is to be a 'phased' reopening of schools, where some year groups get to go back to the academic grind, namely P1 to P3, and some secondary school pupils who need to carry out practical assignments (whatever *they* are!).
As it's all about the numbers, I think the First Minister will take a 'wait and see' approach at the next two weekly review. If the numbers look good, then more year groups will return. If *not*, she might hold the frame and keep it to the initial year groups until the next review. I don't think non essential retail has a hope in *hell* of opening back up again, not until a more substantial number of school

children have been safely set up in the schools. Just my view.
The future of the more 'fun' things, however, does seem a little bit more uncertain.
I think non essential retail may open in our neck of the woods, at the end of March, but restrictions will remain in force, masks, distancing, anything to remind us of how we should be behaving as we speed towards a new normal!
It's truly the hospitality industry I feel sorry for, as well as tourism!
There's a remote chance, I feel, that pubs and licensed premises generally, will open round about June, but, don't get all excited peeps! I'm guessing you'll only get as far as the, soon to be ironically named, *Beer Garden*! Because, in the recent tradition of being treated like five year olds, you won't be trusted with alcohol! Just an orange juice, or, if you're feeling adventurous, a *lemonade* with a slice of lemon in it! Nobody's getting to see the interior of a pub or bar this year! And, if, by chance, you actually *do*, government guidance will insist upon you sitting five feet away from your drinking buddy, and have you all kitted out like you were about to audition as an extra for a rubbish, low budget drama about a nuclear holocaust or a radiation leak at a power station! Cutlery and plates will be disinfected within an *inch* of their lives, I'm not sure if they'll go down the route of disposable

cutlery and plates! There'll be hand sanitiser in amongst the condiments, so I would be *very* careful that you didn't get *that* mixed up with the vinegar! It would *ruin* your chips!

Looking at the scheduling of special occasions, and indoor gatherings generally, I would exercise caution about booking a special occasion or event at *any* point this year, because, any occasion that is allowed to go ahead, will be *severely* limited on numbers. A nightmare for anyone compiling a guest list of any description, and it could lose you friends *forever*! And, as mask wearing *will* be *mandatory*, no escaping that little doozy, the photos of the event aren't going to be too stellar!

Might be worth waiting a bit longer before sorting that out! It wouldn't be so much of a problem, the guest list, if, like me, you don't know a lot of people, but, it's the principle of the thing! So many people had to cancel their weddings because of this, and, with all their data driven bollocks, the government are totally disrespecting everyone by not offering up a conservative estimate, at least, a timeline that they could work with! Good luck with that! It's just an extra layer of control, to not give us any viable estimate or timeline! Data is data, but it *doesn't* help when you have a big event to organise, does it?

Concerts will be a no go area in 2021. Case in point, I got an email advising me that a-ha (aka the

Mighty 'ha!) wouldn't be back on tour till 2022. Luckily, for *me*, before all this Covid crap kicked off, I saw them in Glasgow (baby!), in November 2019! Talk about a close run thing! They were due back on tour, after their December 2019 shows, in March 2020 or thereabouts, but Covid put the kibosh on *that*! I think other bands might do the same, too much of a logistical nightmare to plan gigs without *dates* to work with. See? Dates are every bit as important as their precious data!

So, with the plug temporarily pulled on the tour, I can see why his pop highness, Sir Morten of Harket, took up the offer to don the mantle of Viking on season 2 of *The Masked Singer*.

Lockdown does strange things to people, and the boredom must have been driving him insane!(For the record, his vocals are still stunning! At *his* age! I am not worthy! I still hope I have mine when I get to his age!).

It's already driving *me* to distraction! Why do you think I'm doing this? (I *still* don't know the answer to that!).

Theatres might reopen, but seating will be dramatically reduced, and I think this may also be the case in cinemas. There won'be 'full houses', because, 'Covid loves a crowd!'

We may also get to see dentists and opticians round about June, maybe July, but, given the backlog of

clients these places will have, I'm not overly optimistic!
I'm not going to pitch in any more at this point, because I feel I'd end up digging a hole for myself! Let's just wait and see if the fledgling vaccination programme delivers the goods, and, with it, *freedom*!

<u>*The Final Thought*</u>

So...been a bit of a whistle stop tour through the ongoing pandemic, hasn'it? But, our journey will soon be at an end! At least, it will be on these pages! Can't make the same promise about the wider world, sadly! Anyway, *just* as I was about to wrap up, well, whatever *this* is, I did have a minor epiphany as I was watching a programme the other night on Channel 5, about wartime Britain, and how we had to *Dig For Victory*, and, *Make Do And Mend*. There were all manner of inspirational campaigns put out by the government at that time to rally the troops, keep people's spirits up, and, most important of all, at *no* point did they ever treat the populace like unruly five year olds who wouldn't eat their greens! Nope, they were addressed like *proper* human beings, equals, equals who were respected enough to be spoken to directly, no sugar coating, snowflaking rubbish! Says a lot about our society, doesn't it? When people will go on Twitter to complain about wilfully misunderstanding an innocent comment someone made, making a federal case of it! What I mean is that, keeping people's spirits up, inspiring them, key things that are a prerequisite in *any* crisis, Wars, Pandemics, etc, this was decidedly lacking, and it still *is* now! Frankly, it's disappointing, and big style shame on our governments for not taking the time to *really* motivate us to keep us sane! Patronising ad campaigns don't cut the mustard with *me*! Treating us like five year olds instead of as adults, and equals! Offering *nothing* but the occasional 'Stick with it!' Yeah, that'll help us hold the frame till it's all under control! In *fact*, using us as a filtering system to be deployed when explaining to our children, those of us who have them, why they can't go round to their friends houses, why they had to be shut in all year, near enough, because *they* right royally screwed up! They just don't think of the human cost! I say that it's not too late! They need to get the people onside, or the NHS will collapse under the weight of lockdown related mental health cases! Covid won't get a look in! You *have* to admit that condescending commercials will only further compound the problem! They need to ramp up the 'rah! rah! rah!' let their people *know* that their efforts are appreciated, without couching the insultingly mild

encouragement in a command, like, 'Roll up our sleeves!'in a bid to promote greater uptake of the vaccine! It's a no from me! It doesn't come across in these *boring* fortnightly parliamentary reviews! They don't set aside *any* part of their monologues for motivational speaking! I only advise this because I want to offset a much bigger problem! *Post Lockdown Syndrome*! The snowflakes will *love* that! (Twitter is ready when *you* are!). Coming to a GP surgery near *you*!
And so...my work is *done*!
Here's to 2022, to *normality*, and all of its glory!
I'll be seeing you...